C000273202

HAPPINESS

An Hachette UK Company
www.hachette.co.uk

First published in Great Britain in 2020 by Pyramid,
an imprint of Octopus Publishing Group Ltd
Carmelite House, 50 Victoria Embankment,
London EC4Y 0DZ
www.octopusbooks.co.uk

Distributed in the US by
Hachette Book Group
1290 Avenue of the Americas
4th and 5th Floors
New York, NY 10104

Distributed in Canada by
Canadian Manda Group
664 Annette St.
Toronto, Ontario, Canada M6S 2C8

ISBN 978-0-7537-3430-8

A CIP catalogue record for this book is available from the British Library

Printed and bound in China

10 9 8 7 6 5 4 3 2 1

Publisher: Lucy Pessell
Designer: Hannah Coughlin
Editor: Sarah Kennedy
Editorial Assistant: Emily Martin
Production Managers: Lucy Carter and Nic Jones
Image credit: Pamela Nhlengethwa/Unsplash

Some of this material was previously published in *365 Ways to a Simple, Spritual Life* by Madonna Gauding.

HAPPINESS

INTRODUCTION

WHAT IS HAPPINESS?

HAPPINESS (noun):

1. The quality or state of being happy.
2. Good fortune; pleasure; contentment; joy.

We live in the most complex culture in history, and we probably experience more activity and devour more information in one day than our ancestors did in a lifetime. And all this takes place in an intense electromagnetic haze of marketing, advertising and entertainment. We may have acquired a lot of 'stuff' and lead very stimulating lives, but real happiness and contentment are often eluding us. In fact, countless numbers of us are sleep-deprived, over-extended and deeply in debt; and stress-related diseases are rampant.

Somewhere along the line we have confused standard of living with quality of life. And clearly they are not the same.

Increasingly, scientists and philosophers are exploring what true happiness actually is and how we can achieve it. If happiness were a formula, it would perhaps look something like this:

GRATITUDE
+
LOVE
+
MINDFULNESS
+
ACHIEVABLE GOALS
=
HAPPINESS

Variations of this are coloured by subjective opinion. The one thing most happiness researchers do seem to agree on is that happiness is a choice: something that comes from within and that you can strive to achieve, regardless of your circumstances.

The road to a balanced and happy life is different for each of us, though there are some generic things we can all ask ourselves. Ask yourself:

- What makes me truly happy?
- What qualities do I want to embody?
- How do I want to feel – emotionally, physically and spiritually – on a daily basis?
- What work would be most fulfilling, regardless of the pay cheque?
- Are my possessions serving me or are they burdening me?

- How can I feel more connected to nature, to the people in my life and to my spiritual practice?

- What do I want to do before I die?

- What do I need to heal?

When you find your answers to these questions, they will provide you with a blueprint for a life that's no longer driven by external pressures. You will have set your life on a course that is internally guided by your highest motives and deepest values, and which is uniquely and authentically yours.

HAPPINESS IS A CHOICE

Hold on to that. The happiest people do not seek happiness in other people or possessions. They are not held hostage by circumstance. They understand that happiness comes from within and it is a choice.

Today, whatever is going on in your life, choose happiness.

“THE GREATEST PART OF OUR HAPPINESS DEPENDS ON OUR DISPOSITIONS, NOT OUR CIRCUMSTANCES.”

MARTHA WASHINGTON

CHOOSE YOUR PATH

We are all unique individuals on our own journey. You are, and always will be, a work in progress.

Commit to simplifying your life and mastering whatever makes you happy, and you will begin an exciting lifelong journey that will put you firmly in control of your own destiny.

TAKE YOUR TIME, AND DON'T FORGET TO BE KIND TO YOURSELF ALONG THE WAY

START SMALL

To achieve happiness on a smaller scale, it's important to first address the things you can do on a daily basis. Our brains love achieving goals big and small, and simple everyday tasks are no exception. Try the daily objectives that follow in this section – you'll notice the difference sooner than you might think.

FOCUSING ON SMALL WINS CAN BREAK DOWN SEEMINGLY UNACHIEVABLE AIMS

GET SOME SUNLIGHT

We all feel better when the sun comes out, but sunlight is one of the most overlooked keys to good health.

Unfortunately, too much living indoors, has kept us from enjoying its benefits. Sunlight benefits your bones, lowers your cholesterol and blood pressure, and wards off depression. Our bodies need 400 units of vitamin D a day – you can get that by exposing your face to sunlight for 15 minutes.

For better health and increased happiness, be sure to get a little sunlight each day.

EAT WELL

Indulge in mood-boosting nutrients to improve your mental state as well as your physical wellbeing. Studies have suggested that happiness and mental wellbeing are highest among people who eat plenty of fruit and vegetables every day.

When you're on the go, and you eat on the run, it's easy to skip your vegetables. But you may have forgotten how healthful, delicious and interesting they can be.

Get a good cookbook and experiment with vegetables you don't normally cook. You're probably familiar with broccoli, romaine lettuce and cauliflower, but what about rapini, kolhrabi and bitter melon?

EXERCISE

Exercise increases endorphins and other feel-good brain chemicals, so get moving today. Research suggests that the mood benefits of just 20 minutes of exercise can last for 12 hours. In fact exercise has such a profound effect on our happiness and wellbeing that it is an effective strategy for overcoming depression. If you aren't able to join a gym or health club, there are plenty of other ways to get moving.

Some suggestions are: ride your bicycle to work; walk short distances instead of driving; use the stairs instead of elevators; or do some gardening as a form of exercise. Check out your neighbourhood parks for walking and running tracks – some of them include stations for doing chin-ups or other exercises. And inexpensive exercise balls are great for home use.

EXPRESS YOURSELF

Many of us suppress our feelings in order to keep the peace with others. This is so restrictive and can lead to a mediocre existence.

Have the strength to express your feelings. Have the courage to live the way you want to.

"THE BEST DAY OF YOUR LIFE IS THE ONE ON WHICH YOU DECIDE YOUR LIFE IS YOUR OWN. NO APOLOGIES OR EXCUSES."

BOB MOAWAD

STAND UP FOR YOURSELF

Trust in yourself and your own instincts. Don't shy away from defending your actions. Have conviction in your opinions and behavior, and don't let anybody talk you into or out of situations.

IMPROVE YOUR SLEEP

We all know that sleep helps the body to repair itself, increases focus and concentration, but did you know it also plays an important role in happiness? Scientific studies have proven that sleep affects our sensitivity to negative emotions. So if you want to be more resilient, get an early night.

Getting a good night's sleep is key to productivity and happiness the next day.

Create an environment in your bedroom that is as serene and relaxing as possible, and aim for 7–9 hours a night.

TURN OFF THE TV

Television has its redeeming values, but mostly it bombards us with images of conflict, violence and exploitation.

Try cutting down TV time gradually by substituting other activities that you find enjoyable. Have a family games night, take the dog for a walk in the park or read a book. Have days with no television.

HAVE A LAUGH

Laughter improves health, mood and social skills, and is now even used as a therapy (laughter yoga was started in Mumbai by Dr Maden Katarina, who is now happily running over 5,000 clubs worldwide). So raise those endorphin levels and have a good chuckle, whether that's by watching a funny film or just being a bit silly.

"MOST OF US WOULD BE UPSET IF WE WERE ACCUSED OF BEING SILLY. BUT THE WORD 'SILLY' COMES FROM THE OLD ENGLISH WORD 'SELIG', MEANING 'TO BE BLESSED, HAPPY, HEALTHY AND PROSPEROUS'."

ZIG ZIGLAR

MEDITATE

Take 10 minutes out of your day for a mindfulness meditation.

Being mindful means living in the moment, noticing what's going on both within our minds and in our immediate surroundings. It involves a gentle, non-judgemental acceptance of thoughts.

Instead of worrying about what has been and what is yet to come, ground yourself in the present moment and appreciate what is right here, right now. Take three deep breaths and realize that you are here, you are alive and all is well. Notice your thoughts, but don't judge them. Let them float away for five minutes as you focus on your breathing and just "being."

TAKE A FIVE-MINUTE BREAK

You may work for three or four hours at your computer without getting up. When you finally stop, you're exhausted. Although you may be working long hours, you may not be as productive as you think.

Take five minutes out of every hour to stand up and stretch. Then gently palm your eyes and rub your temples. Take a few deep breaths, and if possible take a short walk. You'll be much more productive, and healthier both physically and mentally, at the end of the day.

COMMUNICATE IN PERSON

With access to round-the-clock and instantaneous communication by mobile phone and email, it's easy to put off visiting someone when you can talk, or email, as often as you like. But it's important to make time to see your friends and family in person.

Don't rely on email and phones as a substitute for communicating with someone in person. Make time in your life to be with the people you love.

NOTICE THE LITTLE THINGS

Bringing your full attention to bear on whatever you're doing is essential to all accomplishments, however lofty or mundane. It's a skill that takes practice, and it's developed with effort. Many self-help books recommend multi-tasking – reading while you eat, watching TV while you cook, reading and answering emails while talking on the phone. However, no one wrote a symphony while making dinner.

Breathe deeply for a few moments before you begin a task. Let go of all thoughts, except those that pertain to what you are about to do. Bring all your intention to focus on the work before you. Notice whether you feel more interested in life when you practise single-minded attention on the task in hand.

BE GRATEFUL

Being grateful for and celebrating all the small things in your life can be a real mood booster.

Write down three good things that happened to you in the past week – it doesn't matter how small it was. This is a great way to ground yourself in what you love about your life.

GRATEFUL PEOPLE ARE INEVITABLY MORE FULFILLED, CONTENTED AND HAPPY

SMILE

Several studies have shown that smiling may not just be an outward manifestation of a happy feeling. It may actually be able to cause a happy feeling.

The next time you're feeling down, try smiling at someone – or to yourself – to lift your mood.

SURROUND YOURSELF WITH HAPPY PEOPLE

Happiness is catching. Being around contented people boosts your own mood. And being happy yourself, you give something back to them – one big reciprocal circle of happy.

"HAPPINESS IS LETTING GO OF WHAT YOU THINK YOUR LIFE IS SUPPOSED TO LOOK LIKE AND CELEBRATING IT FOR EVERYTHING THAT IT IS."

MANDY HALE

THE BIGGER PICTURE

In order to find true and lasting happiness, it is important to address the bigger picture. What lifestyle changes can you make? What bad habits can you kick? How can you change the way you think?

This section looks at how to achieve meaningful and lasting happiness.

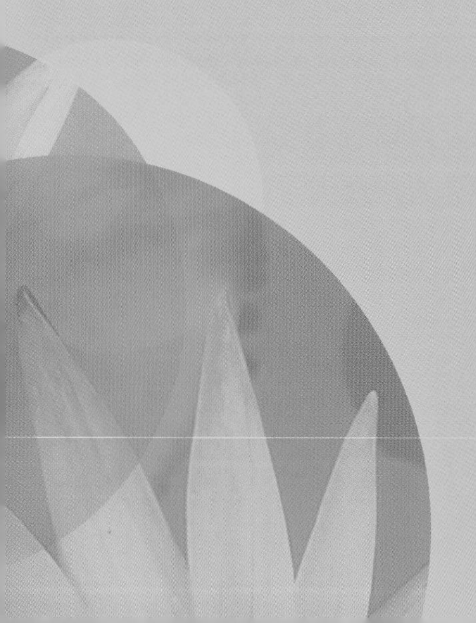

RISK BEING WHO YOU ARE

Social and family pressures sometimes cause us to suppress and deny our true natures. You may be in a profession that is socially acceptable and pleases your family, but has nothing to do with what you really want to do.

The important thing is to risk expressing what you're not articulating in your life, because to not do so means you are denying yourself the joy of authentic living.

APPRECIATE WHAT YOU HAVE

The trick to having a positive mind, even in the worst of times, is to focus on what's going right for you. When you feel you don't have everything you need, it's easy to discount your blessings. When you don't have money for the rent, and the bills are piling up – even though it may be difficult – focus on what you do have. Be sure to consider non-material wealth: your family and friends, your health, your education, your talents and your values. Then focus on the material wealth you do have (however small).

"THAT MAN IS RICHEST WHOSE PLEASURES ARE CHEAPEST."

HENRY DAVID THOREAU

BE YOURSELF

Don't feel that you have to conform to your peer group. Wear what makes you feel good regardless of whether or not it's in fashion, listen to the music you like, watch the movies you love, read the books that inspire you. It's only when you are true to yourself in this way that you become comfortable in your own skin and so can live a full and courageous life.

DON'T BE A CONSUMER

Shopping is part of our modern way of life. But it's important to remind yourself that you are not a consumer. Your importance as a human being is not measured by your buying power, or by the sophistication of your carefully researched choices. Your value is not measured by the cut of your clothes, by the car you drive or by the brand of anything you buy.

For one week, don't go shopping. Try creating something instead. You could plant your own herbs, write a poem, make a drawing or bake something from scratch.

LET GO OF BEING A PASSIVE CONSUMER AND EMBRACE YOURSELF AS A MAKER AND A CREATIVE BEING.

MAKE EVERY ACT COUNT

Contemplate the shortness of your life and find a renewed appreciation of the importance of every moment. With that appreciation, make better choices and more conscious decisions about how you spend your time.

Stop doing things that don't fit with who you are and what you want to be.

At the end of your day, look over what you did from this perspective: What actions were best left undone, and which actions contributed to your life?

HAVE SELF-RESPECT

When you look in the mirror, do you have respect for the person staring back at you? Are you living your life with dignity, in line with the values you want to uphold? If you can't answer 'yes', ask yourself why not. What would you have to do to regain your self-respect?

Perhaps you're doing work that pays well, but ultimately harms other people. If so, try to find more positive employment. If you're in a relationship that is demeaning, leave it. If you have an addiction, get help. If you harmed someone, make amends. Self-respect takes self-love, self-compassion and ongoing maintenance.

LOVE THE BODY YOU HAVE

One of the keys to a simpler life is accepting yourself as you are. Reduce your stress and anxiety by the simple act of loving yourself. Because social pressures to be thin are rampant, it's especially important to love the body you have.

First of all, don't put yourself down. Concentrate on how your body feels, rather than how it looks. Be active: walk, run, do yoga, dance.

Look into the mirror and love the person looking back at you.

ACCEPT PRAISE

A huge part of becoming a more confident, courageous and happy person lies in accepting praise. When somebody praises you for something, don't discredit them as is so often our natural stock response. Instead, accept compliments with grace and openness. Let other people's positive assessment of you motivate you to suceed.

RECOGNIZE IMPERMANENCE

Nothing lasts. When you ignore this fact, you cause yourself to suffer. Impermanence is a part of life – from smaller, less impactful losses to the larger life-changing ones, such as the death of a loved one. But consider that, without impermanence, a flower wouldn't blossom, the rain wouldn't fall, the sun wouldn't rise in the morning or set in the evening.

Meditate on the reality of impermanence. Think about your life a year ago and how you have changed for better or worse since then.

GET RID OF GUILT

Guilt is a useless emotion. You can become stuck in guilt and shame, and even make it part of your identity. Yet it doesn't necessarily lead you to change your behaviour or make you a better person. Regret, on the other hand, is a more positive emotion. It allows you to focus on your actions, and moves you towards change and healing.

First, if you caused someone harm, acknowledge it. Then express sincere regret for having hurt them. Let them know this is not the way you want to behave. If possible, do something to make amends.

REDEFINE SUCCESS

Our culture's definition of success is fairly limited. The signs are mostly external: a high-paying job, a nice car, beautiful clothes, a beautiful partner and a large home.

Consider these alternative definitions of success, which don't require conspicuous consumption: you have a successful life if you have a safe place to live, good health, a nurturing family life, ongoing education, spiritual development, good friends, and work that feeds you emotionally and intellectually. You're a successful person if you are capable of giving and receiving love and experiencing joy.

WHAT DO YOU CONSIDER
TO BE THE INGREDIENTS
OF A SUCCESSFUL LIFE?
MORE IMPORTANTLY, HOW
DO YOU MEASURE SUCCESS
FOR YOURSELF?

ACCEPT CHANGE

If you find yourself dreading or avoiding change, you may be cheating yourself out of new and wonderful opportunities.

Are you afraid to take a great new job because it means moving to a new city? Are you scared to leave an unhealthy relationship because you're terrified to be alone? The nature of life is change, and nothing ever stays the same.

If you're afraid of change in a particular situation, identify exactly what you're afraid of and list three actions you can take to alleviate your fears.

CREATE TRUE WEALTH

When we think of wealth, we usually think of material wealth, freedom from financial worry or a beautiful home. But this is not an adequate definition of true wealth. Money is just one element in a system that makes up a good life.

Do you have a vision for your life and spiritual values? These intangibles are part of your wealth as well. Do you participate in various communities – professional or recreational? These wonderful people enrich you with support and companionship. Do you enjoy the place in which you live? Do you partake of its amenities, such as parks and libraries? Generate a sense of gratitude for all aspects of your wealth.

DECIDE HOW YOU'RE GOING TO LIVE

At least once a year ask yourself if you're living the life you want to be living. Have you made clear and conscious decisions about your friends and lovers, your work, what kind of house you live in, what part of the world you call home, and what spiritual path you've chosen?

Ask yourself what you would do if you could do anything your heart desired. If you've simply never thought about what you really want, write down what your ideal life would look like. Describe a typical day. Where would you be living, who would be with you, what work would you be doing?

Today, make yourself a promise that you will not compare yourself to anyone else. You will not dwell on your flaws. Make a list of all the positive things about your personality to remind yourself that you are a good, kind human being. Being kinder to yourself will hugely increase your wellbeing. This is how you are going to live.

"LIFE ISN'T ABOUT FINDING YOURSELF. LIFE IS ABOUT CREATING YOURSELF."

GEORGE BERNARD SHAW

COMMIT TO CHANGE

Change of any kind can be exciting or frightening. The fun kind we pursue; the frightening kind we tend to put off.

If you need to quit smoking, lose weight or leave a relationship, let the reality sink in. Let any feelings emerge – fear, anger or whatever else is on your mind.

Then mentally close the door of the past behind you. Now you're going to go forward, one step at a time, and change what you have to change. If you have to stop smoking, develop a plan: see your doctor, get a prescription, sign up at a stop-smoking clinic. If you have to end a relationship, get support from a friend or therapist.

ONCE YOU COMMIT TO CHANGE, YOUR FEAR AND ANGER WILL LESSEN, AND YOUR HOPE AND ENERGY WILL INCREASE

BE A BEGINNER

As children we were unafraid to climb the tallest tree or fling ourselves down treacherous slopes in a toboggan, yet once we reach adulthood life has taught us to be fearful of many things.

The sensible "what if" part of our brain kicks in and inhibits us in ways that it didn't when we were children. Our knowledge of everything that could go wrong holds us back. Try to embrace the Zen Buddhism concept of "a beginner's mind" by having the enthusiastic, curious, open mind of a child. Question what you would do if you weren't afraid.

“WE DON’T STOP PLAYING BECAUSE WE GROW OLD; WE GROW OLD BECAUSE WE STOP PLAYING.”

GEORGE BERNARD SHAW

PRACTISING KINDNESS

Research has shown that altruistic behaviour releases endorphins in the brain and therefore boosts our own feelings of wellbeing.

In being kinder to others, not only do we help build up trust, community, and empathy within society, we increase our own happiness levels.

KINDNESS IS RECIPROCAL, SO WHAT WE GIVE WE WILL ONE DAY GET BACK IN RETURN.

LISTEN

Instead of waiting to jump in to a conversation, slow down and really listen to what somebody is telling you. You will feel a better connection to the person you are talking to if you understand their views. And a better connection equals increased levels of contentment within a relationship.

BE POLITE

Being polite takes nothing, and can really brighten somebody's day, no matter how small the action. Hold the door open for the person behind you, let someone go in front of you in a line.

Gestures such as these add up to create an enveloping attitude of kindness.

DON'T JUDGE

The more you judge others, the more harshly you tend to judge yourself, so nobody wins from taking this particular standpoint in life. Remember you don't know other people's stories and battles, and you're in no position to judge anyway.

It's also important to accept that all people are different – it's part of what makes our world so wonderfully diverse. It is a very good thing to have conflicting opinions and ideas to others, as this will help you learn and open your mind to different ways of thinking.

SHARE

Very different from giving away things you no longer need, sharing is about giving away a little of something that is meaningful to you, whether it be half of your lunch, your favourite dress you could loan to a friend for a special occasion, or even words of advice.

There are many benefits to sharing. Not only can it bring you closer to family and friends, it's also a great way of starting conversations and getting to know new people.

COMPLIMENT SOMEONE

Think about the last time someone complimented you. It may have been only a short or passing comment, but it probably cheered you up quite a bit!

Make the effort to genuinely compliment at least three people – today and every day. Focus on things as trivial as a new haircut, through to character traits and achievements.

EXPRESS YOUR LOVE

Try saying "I love you" to friends and family a little more often. You never know who may need to hear it. It'll also help to remind yourself how many amazing people you have to be grateful for in your life.

VOLUNTEER

Volunteer to help others in need, perhaps at a homeless shelter serving meals or find an organization the matches your concerns and passions.

If it's hard for you to find the time to volunteer, why not start making regular donations to a few charities of your choice? Or perhaps make regular drop offs at your local food bank.

"IF THOSE WHO OWE US NOTHING GAVE US NOTHING, HOW POOR WE WOULD BE."

ANTONIO PORCHIA

HELP OTHERS

Helping someone less agile than yourself across the road, or to reach something from a high shelf in the supermarket is no great effort for you, but this simple act of kindness could really make a difference to someone else's day.

Maybe buy a stranger their coffee, let someone jump the line ahead of you, send anonymous flowers, buy someone a lottery ticket ... then revel in the warm glow that act of random kindness brings you.

FORGIVE

According to a rapidly growing body of research, holding a grudge and nursing grievances can affect physical as well as mental health.

So learn how to forgive. Try to let go of past hurts. Move on with compassion in your heart and your head held high.

LETTING GO OF THE FEAR OF HUMILIATION, AND OF FEAR ITSELF, WILL ALLOW YOU TO LOVE MORE

LEARN TO LISTEN

It takes effort to listen. More to the point, it takes an open mind and heart. That may be difficult for you to achieve. You may have a hard time trusting and want to protect yourself. Or perhaps no one listened to you when you were a child. However, through active listening, you gain the joy of deep communication with another human being. Practise the art of listening by focusing your attention on the other person.

CULTIVATE COMPASSION

You may think that cultivating compassion is something you do for someone else. But when you generate compassion for others you do it for yourself as well.

When you find yourself in a difficult or stressful situation with someone, regardless of how you feel about them, generate the wish to relieve his or her suffering. By doing this you take your focus off your own distress, and you lessen your own anger or anxiety. As you open your heart to him or her, you make it possible to resolve your differences.

WORK THROUGH YOUR DIFFERENCES

We usually sort people into three piles – friends, enemies and neutrals. On a more subtle level, you may find yourself feeling one up, or one down, with friends, loved ones or those whom you consider 'difficult'. You may find yourself shifting your relationship with people over time. Your previous 'best friend' may now be your enemy, and your one-time enemy may now be your beloved partner. Try to avoid sorting people into categories, or competing for power.

Practise seeing everyone as being just like yourself – that is, wanting to find happiness and trying to avoid suffering. This is the beginning of compassion and kindness.

7 STEPS TO HAPPINESS:

1. Think Less, Feel More

2. Frown Less, Smile More

3. Talk Less, Listen More

4. Judge Less, Accept More

5. Watch Less, Do More

6. Complain Less, Appreciate More

7. Fear Less, Love More

BEING CONTENT WITH THE EVERYDAY

True and lasting happiness doesn't always come from the places we imagine it does. It doesn't come from major changes in your personal circumstances, such as winning the lottery or quitting your job to go travelling. It's all about how you behave on a day-to-day basis, and seeing your life for what it is.

So many people get stuck in the destructive cycle of thinking that there must be more to life than this. Well, there is, and it's right in front you. Today, open your eyes to what's around you. On your walk to work, the shops or wherever you're going, look at the trees around you, the clouds in the sky, a leaf on a bush, the sound of birdsong, children laughing. Wherever you are, there will be something beautiful to tune into.

NECESSITY VS. DESIRE

Take a sheet of paper and write down what you feel are the very basic necessities of life in general. You may have on your list food, shelter, clothing, work, health care, and perhaps a partner or a spiritual life. Next, write down what you feel are the necessities of your life. By now your list has probably expanded considerably. You may have written down a certain standard of shelter, a certain amount of and style of clothing, and perhaps new furniture and a top-of-the-range computer.

After you've listed your necessities, go back over them. Consider each item and ask yourself if it is really a necessity or a desire.

APPRECIATING HOME

Home can mean many things. We yearn to 'go home' – wherever that may be. We get 'homesick'. With some people we feel more 'at home' than with others. We want our house or apartment to 'feel like home'.

What does home mean to you? Do you feel at home in your body? Do you yearn to come home to yourself? If you don't feel at home in your physical dwelling, in your job, your relationship or your city or town, ask why that is so. What changes do you need to make in order to feel at home in your body, your mind and your physical surroundings?

Regularly experiencing positive emotions results in an upward spiral. So start at home and find joy, gratitude, contentment, and inspiration in as many places as you can today. Then more will follow.

"HOME IS NOT A PLACE, IT'S A FEELING."

CECELIA AHERN

KEEP YOUR WARDROBE SIMPLE

If you work in an office, you probably have to look good every day, but this doesn't mean you need to have several designer pieces and handbags in order to feel your best.

Classic styles in solid colours can help you look presentable for work in half the time, and they last from season to season. Be sure to buy neutral colours and then build from there. Use scarves and jewellery to change your look, or ties and coloured shirts. The cost savings are significant, and you'll discover how worrying less about what you look like can be truly liberating.

FIND JOY AT WORK

We work primarily for an income. Yet we also work for the approval of others, for a sense of power and mastery, and to be of service to others. But how many of us work to experience joy? It's not so much what you do as how you do it that's the key to joyful work.

Be fully present, at each moment, as you go through your day. You can do this by bringing all your senses and awareness to each task. In other words, regardless of pressure, focus only on what you are doing now. By doing so you'll be less reactive to external demands and interruptions, and more empowered in using your skills and knowledge. You'll also unleash your creativity and problem-solving abilities.

OVERCOME ENVY

It's fairly easy to celebrate a loved one's accomplishments. However, when you have difficulty with someone, you may have a hard time enjoying their successes. You may say 'Congratulations!', but in your heart your words ring hollow. Examine the stories you are telling yourself. Do you wish the other person failure at the same time as you're feeling inadequate? Notice how jealousy and envy hurt you, and cause you misery. Experiment with rejoicing in the face of your envy, and notice how it frees your heart and eases your own suffering.

“COMPARISON IS THE THIEF OF JOY.”

THEODORE ROOSEVELT

APPRECIATE THE JOY OF SIMPLE EATING

If you want to save some serious money, stop 'eating out' in restaurants. Instead, buy groceries and 'eat in'. If that sounds like a prison sentence, you may want to explore some of the positive reasons for cooking and eating at home. First, you'll learn how to cook or be a better cook. Second, you can improve your health by controlling what and how much you eat. No more greasy fast food or huge restaurant portions. Third, you can enjoy gourmet meals without breaking the bank – recreate those special dishes at home. Fourth, you can enjoy low-cost socializing with friends by having pot-luck meals. Fifth, you can potentially save lots of money per year. Now, what's so bad about that?

ENJOY SIMPLE PLEASURES

You may have a preconceived idea of what will bring you pleasure, and then pursue whatever it is that you desire. But one key to a happy life is the ability to appreciate simple pleasures as they arise. It might be the sight of yellow daffodils in a white vase, the beauty of red strawberries against a blue bowl, the taste of home-made bread warm from the oven, or seeing the sunrise in the morning. It might be holding your child as he or she sleeps in your arms, the joy of clean sheets or the relaxation of a warm bath.

Rather than seeking pleasure, the trick is to be present, aware and open to the pleasures all around you.

IT'S OKAY TO WORRY

Even though it may seem like everyone is happy all of the time, it simply isn't true.

If you're human, you worry. What you worry about is unique to you. Instead of worrying as problems arise, try setting aside a regular time to worry. Find a notebook, a pen and a serene spot where you won't be disturbed. List everything you're worried about. Prioritize your worries according to what stresses you out the most. Be sure to stick to whatever schedule you've set for worrying, and limit your worrying at other times. By doing this you'll have much more control over your life and your problems.

DEMATERIALIZE

When you see something you want, you get excited. You research your potential purchase, and weigh up the pros and cons of different models. You think about having it, and a warm glow temporarily fills your body. You know that having this item will make you happy. You comparison-shop locally and online. Finally you make your decision. You buy it and bring it home. It's great! For 24–48 hours, you're in heaven. A week later the item is starting to fade from your consciousness. A month later you have forgotten about it. You've moved on to the next item.

MATERIAL POSSESSIONS CAN BRING YOU TEMPORARY PLEASURE, BUT THEY DON'T LEAD TO HAPPINESS.

MAKE ENJOYMENT YOUR WEALTH

Are you capable of enjoying life in the moment, regardless of what you have or don't have? If you're sipping a cup of coffee right now, savour it. If the sun is setting, take the time to enjoy the display. If you love your new car, enjoy driving it, but know that the car itself isn't making you happy – you are. Enjoyment comes from inside. It's an approach to life that requires a light touch, the ability to bask in the sensual and the capacity to let go – it doesn't require money.

LIVE WITHIN YOUR MEANS

Our culture encourages desires of every kind, 24 hours a day, seven days a week, because encouraging desire sells things.

For one month, avoid all advertising as much as possible. Enjoy – and rejoice in – the possessions you already have. Spend less than you take in and put some money in your savings account. Feeling financially grounded and in control offsets the stress of living beyond your means.

"LIVE A SIMPLE LIFE; YOU WILL OWN THE MOST BEAUTIFUL TREASURES OF THE WORLD."

MEHMET MURAT ILDAN

HAVE THAT DIFFICULT CONVERSATION

If you've been putting off a difficult conversation with a partner, another family member or your boss, it's probably hurting you more than the actual conversation ever could. You may need to end a relationship, bring up the past with an abuser, or raise something equally frightening and challenging.

Before you have the conversation, get help from a counsellor, or consult self-help books. You don't have to go in there without support. Let a close friend or therapist know what you are about to do. After the conversation, be sure you have a friend or counsellor to talk to about your experience.

AFFIRM YOUR COMPLETENESS

We live in cultures where advertising invades our lives 24/7. The message of most advertising is that you're lacking something, and that the product being advertised will make you whole. It's important to overcome that basic message by meditating on your own completeness.

Find a quiet moment and close your eyes. Affirm that you are not an apprentice human being in need of approval by an outside authority. Affirm that you are not lacking in beauty, health or material possessions. Affirm to yourself that you are complete and whole. Affirm to yourself, and the universe, that you are perfect just as you are.

LEARN FROM THE PAST

Dwelling on previous mistakes will only serve to hinder your progress. Today, make the decision to forgive yourself for all of your past failings. You will walk lighter and feel braver if you can do this.

Now bring to mind all the times in your life when you have acted positively or courageously, when you faced your fears and took a leap into the unknown with successful outcomes.

LET POSITIVE PAST EXPERIENCES INSPIRE YOU TO ONCE AGAIN ACT WITH BRAVERY AND OPTIMISM

FOCUS ON THE POSITIVE

When trying to motivate yourself to take the first step in accomplishing a goal, envisage positive outcomes. Focus on how great you would feel, and how improved your life would be instead of getting caught up in thoughts of what might go wrong.

Focus on embracing everything positive that happens to you today, however small that thing may be. For anything negative that happens, turn it into a positive. There's always a new way of looking at something, a way to put a positive spin on it.

DITCH PERFECTIONISM

The quest for perfection is so often what stops us in our tracks before we've even begun. We're afraid that we can't do something perfectly and so we don't even try. Studies have shown that perfectionists actually tend to be less successful people than those who accept setbacks and learn from them. So today let go of the desire to be perfect – it will only ever impede your progress.

DON'T KILL YOUR DREAM

If you have a dream – to paint, to sing, to write as a career – you may have to contend with disapproval from friends and relatives. They may think you're irresponsible, and your aspirations frivolous. They may insist that only certain lifestyles are acceptable: those careers that guarantee the most power and status. However, you have the power to decide what's important to you, and what your responsibilities are.

It's important to hold your own and maintain your dreams. Work out a way to make them happen. Use your creativity to find a way to support yourself and practise your art. If you believe in yourself, then others will too.